Original title:
The Fruit of Life's Garden

Copyright © 2025 Creative Arts Management OÜ
All rights reserved.

Author: Dorian Ashford
ISBN HARDBACK: 978-1-80586-397-7
ISBN PAPERBACK: 978-1-80586-869-9

Embrace of the Harvest Moon

Under the moon, we dance like goofballs,
Twirling around in our comical shawls.
Pumpkins laugh, their faces aglow,
As squirrels plot to steal the show.

Cornstalks whisper wild, silly tales,
Of chickens on bikes and fish with scales.
Harvest season brings laughs and a cheer,
While the moon winks down, 'Come join us here!'

Tapestry of Flora

In a garden where daisies wear hats,
Roses chat with the cheeky bats.
Tulips giggle, it's quite the sight,
As the sunflowers break into a light fight.

Bees buzzing like tiny marines,
Stealing nectar while doing the scenes.
We join in their weird, zany parade,
Amidst petals that giggle, sun-shaded.

Symphony of Senses

Scented breezes play tricks on our nose,
With aromas of berries, who knows where it goes?
Tasting laughter in a fruity delight,
As bananas do somersaults left and right.

Cherries chuckle, swinging with glee,
While oranges sing notes with a zesty spree.
It's a symphony where giggles prevail,
And laughter echoes, an enchanting tale.

Elysian Fields of Green

In fields of green where laughter grows,
Frogs hold ballet shows, in their toadlike clothes.
Under trees with wiggly limbs,
Squirrels play tag with chipmunk whims.

Butterflies flutter like they own the scene,
Dancing on flowers, oh so serene.
With giggles and joy, we run and play,
In green pastures where silliness stays.

Gleanings of Tomorrow

In the patch where laughter grows,
The carrots wear the silliest clothes.
Beets dance with a wig on their head,
Radishes argue about who's well-bred.

Tomatoes giggle, all juicy and red,
While corn keeps secrets that never get said.
Peppers in a salsa, all spicy and ripe,
Join in a conga, they're ready to hype.

Pumpkins in piles, so round and so bright,
Tell jokes to the moon on a starry night.
Zucchinis prank from their leafy abode,
Playing hide and seek on the vegetable road.

So come plant your jokes in this whimsical plot,
Where each seed you sow brings laughter a lot.
Harvest the chuckles, let joy be your tool,
In this garden of fun, we all play the fool.

Elysium Underfoot

In the realm of roots where giggles abound,
The onions are joking; they're never profound.
Garlic is grinning, a pungent delight,
While mushrooms are sneaking a dance in the night.

Across the green meadow, the peas start to roll,
Breaking into laughter, they've found their true goal.
Radishes tease, "We're the coolest on earth!"
While carrots claim fame, for their orange birth.

The cucumbers stretch in a twelve-legged race,
With vines twisting wildly, oh what a chase!
Squash takes a tumble, all plumped with delight,
Making everyone laugh with their squishy might.

So come take a stroll on this colorful ground,
Where humor grows tall and good vibes abound.
In this patch of joy, funny tales intertwine,
Harvest some giggles; they're sweet and divine.

Serene Moments

In the corner, a pear with a grin,
Waves at the apple, who's just a bit thin.
Bananas in pajamas dance on their peels,
While cherries gossip about a plant with good feels.

The lemon rolls eyes at the peach's smooth skin,
Sour friends are funny, they just want to win.
Watermelon giggles, splashing seeds in the air,
While grapes throw a party, with snacks to share.

Tender Blossoms

Petals fluttering like they're shy,
Sunflowers stand tall, trying to fly.
Roses wear hats made of morning dew,
While daisies play peek-a-boo, just for you.

The violets whisper secrets sweet,
Joking about bees that light on their feet.
Lilies with laughter, a dance on the breeze,
While tulips tease fuss, just to please.

Essence of Sunlit Memories

A squirrel drops acorns like little bombs,
Nature's orchestra playing chaotic psalms.
The sunbeams tickle the grass, oh so bright,
As critters celebrate their antics in flight.

Butterflies wearing polka dots and stripes,
Flinging their colors without any gripes.
The clouds begin teasing with their fluffy tails,
While breezes carry whispers of whimsical tales.

Nature's Brushstrokes

The painter's palette drips in delight,
A canvas of colors, both day and night.
Trees act as brushes, swaying with grace,
Painting laughter on every leaf's face.

The wind blows softly, a giggling spree,
Tickling creatures beneath the old tree.
Mushrooms pop up in their silly hats,
While crickets break into spontaneous chats.

Harvested Resilience

In the fields, the pumpkins wear charming frowns,
While squash jokes about silly royal crowns.
Corn stands tall, making everyone laugh,
As cucumbers stretch just to show off their half.

The scarecrow dances, not quite in control,
While rabbits sneak in, trying to steal the whole bowl.
But laughter rings out as they frolic around,
In this whimsical place, joy knows no bound.

Flourishing Fables

In a patch of green, the veggies play,
Tomatoes wear hats, in a silly way.
Carrots tell jokes that make them laugh,
While peas are at work, plotting a gaffe.

Cucumbers dance with a rhythm so fine,
While radishes roast under sun's bright shine.
The humor grows deep like roots underground,
In this crazy garden, joy is profound.

Seeds of Tomorrow

Planting a seed, what could it be?
A pickle or pumpkin, maybe a pea?
The squirrels hold meetings, debating their fate,
As they plot their next snack—oh, what a state!

Worms in the soil are spinning their tunes,
While insects debate under light of the moons.
With laughter and chatter, they harvest the sun,
In this wild little world, life's never quite done.

Blossoms in the Breeze

Petunias gossip when the wind starts to blow,
Sharing the tales that most wouldn't know.
Daisies and daisies, they gossip with flair,
While sunflowers sashay with pollen to spare.

A butterfly flutters, donning a frown,
"Why'd you all giggle? I flew upside down!"
But petals just chuckle, they've seen it before,
In this floral ensemble, there's always more.

Harvests of Heart and Soul

Gathering fruits as the day starts to fade,
Cherries are squabbling over who gets made.
Bananas stand tall, claiming their supreme,
While oranges argue, "We're part of the team!"

In every basket, there's laughter and cheer,
A melon cracked jokes that everyone could hear.
With harvest in hand, they throw a grand feast,
In this wacky orchard, joy never ceased.

Fragrant Echoes

In the orchard, apples grin,
Laughing as the squirrels spin.
Pears declare a juicy race,
While bananas slip with grace.

Cherries giggle, red and round,
Hiding secrets in the ground.
Peaches waltz, so plump and bold,
Nature's jesters, bright and gold.

Blossoming Journeys

Lemons wearing frowny faces,
Try to win a place in races.
Oranges dance, a zesty crew,
While berries blush in morning dew.

A funky melon rolls along,
Singing silly fruitcake song.
Grapes unite, a cluster cheer,
Life's a feast; grab a cold beer!

Nature's Symphony

Cantaloupes create a beat,
With rhythm fresh, they can't be beat.
Avocados hum a mellow tune,
While limes make jokes under the moon.

Kiwis strum on rusty strings,
While sweet figs show off their bling.
Cucumbers whisper, "Join the fun,"
Their pickles ready, day is done.

Mosaic of Seasons

Winter fruits all dressed in frost,
Yelling, "Who's the boss?"
Spring brings colors, wild and free,
Bouncing bees sing 'Let it be!'

Summer's berries blast a tune,
Underneath the blazing moon.
Fall's pumpkins chuckle, round and stout,
As cider makes us laugh out loud.

Whispers of Nature's Bounty

Beneath the trees, the squirrels plot,
With acorns stolen, they laugh a lot.
Ripe apples dangle, looking so sweet,
While the bees buzz round, making a feat.

Oh, nature's laughter is hard to ignore,
Fruit juice rivers flowing from every door.
A watermelon sings with a juicy grin,
As the garden party is about to begin!

Colors of Abundance

The grapes wear caps like party hats,
Dancing around, inviting the cats.
Lemons chuckle in bright yellow rays,
While cherries gossip about sunny days.

A rainbow spilled in a garden plot,
Juggling colors, a lively shot.
Each berry tells a tale of glee,
In this circus where all are free!

Ripened Dreams

Peaches blush in their fuzzy gowns,
While pumpkins roll and practice frowns.
Strawberries giggle, their seeds on display,
Telling jokes in a very sweet way.

Bananas slip in a playful glide,
While cucumbers joke, showing their pride.
In this dream of fruit, let laughter reign,
For every crunch brings joy, not pain!

Nectar of Existence

Mangoes beam like sunshine blobs,
Cabbage plays doctor, giving out sobs.
Oranges jive to a tangy beat,
While radishes stomp their little feet.

Citrus fruits steal the show with zest,
Pineapples wear crowns, feeling blessed.
Each bite's a giggle, a burst of cheer,
As we feast on madness, year after year!

Fruits of Friendship

With cherries bright, we share a laugh,
Bananas slip, a silly gaffe.
Pineapples dance in zesty cheer,
Lemons squeeze out all our fear.

Grapes giggle in a bunch so tight,
Mangoes flirt, what a delight!
In this orchard, joy will bloom,
Friendship's stew, always in bloom.

Lullabies Beneath the Canopy

Underneath the leafy shade,
Berries sing, a sweet parade.
Oranges hum their sleepy tunes,
While apples play with silver spoons.

In slumber, every fruity friend,
Dreams of pie that never end.
Coconuts with gentle sway,
Lullabies for a sunny day.

Aroma of the Unseen

Peaches whisper secrets rare,
Nutmeg's scent fills the air.
A whiff of joy, a hint of cheer,
As fruit confetti draws us near.

Zesty breezes weave and sway,
Fragrant laughter leads the way.
With every smell, a giggle stirs,
As nature's jokes bring out the purrs.

Indigo and Ivy

Indigo fans with a twisty grin,
Dancing sprouts, let the fun begin.
Ivy climbs with a cheeky pose,
Tickling toes with playful prose.

Blueberries plan a springtime jest,
Laughing hard at the silly quest.
In this patch of vibrant glee,
Discover life's sweet jubilee.

Kaleidoscope of Colors

In the garden where veggies play,
Carrots hide from sun's bright ray.
Tomatoes gossip, laughing loud,
While cabbage wears a leafy shroud.

Radishes blush with every glance,
Peas perform a daring dance.
Cucumbers creep and slyly grin,
"Join our fun!" they wheeze and spin.

Beets are busy, painting dreams,
In berry bowls, the chaos teems.
Lettuce leans to catch a breeze,
Pineapple twirls, aiming to please.

With every seed, a tale begins,
In this patch, everyone wins.
So grab your fork, come take a bite,
In this garden, life's a delight!

Seasons of Strength

Spring sprouts laughter, plants awake,
Turnips wiggle, all for fun's sake.
As summer sizzles, sunflowers cheer,
Zucchini races, "I'm the top tier!"

Autumn arrives, ready to bake,
Pumpkin pie, for goodness' sake!
While winter chills, but don't be blue,
Carrots keep warm with a cozy crew.

With each season, laughter sprouts,
Broccoli giggles, no room for doubts.
Nature's humor, what a sight,
In every crunch, pure delight!

Hidden Orchard Secrets

Underneath the apple tree,
Secrets whisper, wild and free.
Peaches chuckle, ripe and round,
"Find us first!" their voices sound.

Berries hide just out of sight,
In the bushes, what a fright!
Plums tell tales of summer's fun,
While cherries always strike a pun.

Crisp and juicy, nature's score,
Hiding treasures, wanting more.
In this orchard, fun takes flight,
Each bite's a giggle, pure delight!

Nectar of Nostalgia

Sweet memories in every sip,
Lemonade on a summer trip.
Watermelons tease with every bite,
Childhood laughter, pure delight.

Pineapple hats bounce on the grass,
"I'm the king!" they proudly pass.
Fruits unite in a festive race,
Who knew dessert could be such a chase?

Mangoes twirl, a dance so grand,
In this fiesta, join the band.
Taste the nostalgia, set it free,
In every fruit, a memory.

Constellation of Floral Whispers

In a patch of daisies, we play hide and seek,
Bees buzzing loudly, their antics so cheeky.
Sunflowers take selfies, striking a pose,
While the carrots gossip, tipping their toes.

Tulips wearing hats, how absurd and grand,
Juggling ripe strawberries with a delicate hand.
Roses tell puns while the vines weave a song,
Laughter erupts, this garden can't be wrong.

The daisies laugh loud, creating a fuss,
While the potatoes form a small circus bus.
With every new bloom, a new joke is spun,
In this floral cosmos, life's always fun.

As petals confide, and roots intertwine,
Their secrets and laughter flow like sweet wine.
Underneath leafy arches, we prance with delight,
In this universe of blooms, every day feels right.

Tending to Dreams

I planted my wishes beside all my fears,
In the soil of chuckles, watered with tears.
Growing tall and silly, Dreams dance in the breeze,
Tickled by sunbeams, swaying with ease.

Gardening isn't all about labor and toil,
Sometimes it means finding joy in the soil.
Planting potatoes with silly little hats,
Turns work into laughter, and joy into chats.

Watering giggles and weeding the gloom,
Each seed holds a dream, ready to bloom.
With every pluck of a rogue, thorny vine,
I sow up the fun—it's all by design.

So here's to the harvest of chuckles and cheer,
Where we gather our stories, each one so dear.
With friends in the garden, oh what a scene,
We nurture our spirits, we grow as a team.

Arcadia of Abundance

Under the shade of a giant blue fig,
Lies a timid little radish, doing a jig.
Tomatoes chuckle and their seeds take flight,
In this land of plenty, everything feels right.

Pumpkins wear glasses and read lawn care books,
While garlic gives pep talks to the shy little crooks.
Zucchini debates with the proud parsley,
While peas roll their eyes, saying, "You're so sassy!"

Every harvest is filled with giggles and zest,
In a hoedown of harvest, we all feel blessed.
With each carrot pull and turnip unearthing,
We celebrate abundance, with fun and mirth-ing.

So grab a sweet melon and give it a hug,
Join hands with the veggies, let's dance: how smug!
In this playful Arcadia, with joy overflowing,
Each moment is ripe and our laughter keeps growing.

Orchard of Wonder

In the orchard of wonder, apples wear capes,
Chasing around pears, making ridiculous shapes.
Nutty squirrels giggle, with acorns in tow,
Planning a heist on the grinning old crow.

Plums tell tall tales of days gone past,
While cherries throw parties, cheers coming fast.
Beneath the green boughs, secrets galore,
With oranges tart, reminding us more.

Each fruit has a story, a punchline or two,
Bananas slip-slide, a comedic debut.
In this orchard of wonder, life's spherical cheer,
With every new harvest, there's laughter near.

So join in the fun, take a jump and a twirl,
Where laughter and sweetness in chaos unfurl.
In this realm of delight, it's never too late,
To dance through the branches; we'll all celebrate.

Harvest of Whispers

In the orchard's shade, secrets play,
Nuts have no sense, they laugh all day.
Cherries giggle when raindrops fall,
Peaches roll over, having a ball.

Squirrels gossip and give me advice,
"Eat your greens, they're not so nice!"
Lemons pull faces, all sour and bright,
While grapes are just tipsy on vine in the night.

Blossoms of Tomorrow

Daisies dance under the sun's beam,
While radishes plot how to prank the cream.
Tulips wink at the bumblebee,
Saying, "Buzz off, we're not your tea!"

Tomorrow's blooms hide behind the vine,
Dreaming of rainbows and jellybean wine.
Fountains of laughter spill from the bees,
Flowers gossip and rustle the leaves.

Secrets in a Seed

In every tiny seed, a secret lies,
An avocado dreams of becoming fries.
Tomatoes wish they could wear a hat,
While carrots hope to look like a brat.

Peas in a pod are a giggling crew,
Plotting how to make soup askew.
Pumpkins are counting their rich orange dreams,
Imagining pies, with whipped cream themes.

Nectar of Existence

Honey drips down like a sticky joke,
Bees wear shades, and they never choke.
Raspberries tease with their velvety charm,
While prunes giggle, no cause for alarm.

Insects in tuxedos dance in delight,
Their disco moves a comical sight.
Bananas slip into a laugh or two,
While apples say, "Let's brew a fondue!"

Pantheon of Petals

In a world where flowers chat,
Roses claim they're where it's at.
Lilies giggle, sipping dew,
While daisies wear their best perfume.

Sunflowers dance with silly grace,
Giggling bugs join in the race.
Tulips tease the morning light,
Saying, 'Watch us bloom! What a sight!'

When bees arrive, they buzz around,
Chasing gossip near the ground.
'Have you heard? A new bloom's here!'
'Call the petals, bring the cheer!'

In this garden, joy's the rule,
Where every wilted leaf can drool.
So come and join this petal prank,
We'll laugh it up, give thanks, and flank.

Essence of Earth

A carrot once wore a fancy hat,
Said, 'I'm the king!' but felt quite flat.
Tomatoes rolled their eyes with glee,
'You look like you came from a tree!'

The potatoes played a raucous game,
Of who could go and hide with fame.
Zucchini tried to steal the show,
But tripped on squash – oh, what a blow!

Radishes rapped with beats so fresh,
While peppers danced, all in a mesh.
'Let's spice it up!' they all agreed,
And baked a pie—a veggie breed!

So gather 'round this earthy crew,
Where laughter grows, and fun is new.
In this patch of joy unearth,
We find the essence of true mirth.

Woven in Sunlight

The sunbeams tickle leaves on trees,
They giggle, wiggle in the breeze.
Bees wear shades, they're looking cool,
While shadows dance, playing the fool.

Cucumbers roll in a sunlit race,
While broccoli strikes a silly pose face.
Carrots tumble, losing their grip,
All in good fun, no need to trip!

The sunlight paints a golden smile,
As fruits form bonds and chat awhile.
Bananas, grinning, peel with flair,
While cherries giggle without a care.

A cordial party, soft and bright,
Where every veggie shines with light.
In nature's laugh, we find our cheer,
Woven in sunlight, year after year.

Harvesting Moments

With baskets full of giggles, we roam,
In gardens where all good things call home.
Carrots grunt as they pull their weight,
Corn giggles, saying, 'Is it too late?'

Pumpkins pose, feeling so grand,
'Look at us, we're in demand!'
But one rolled off—oh what a twist!
'Hey, that wasn't on my harvest list!'

As apples share their shining glee,
They toss out jokes, all in spree.
Lemons squirt with zestful mirth,
Spreading smiles across the earth.

In every nook, moments are sprung,
We'll tie our laughter, leaf and tongue.
So join the harvest, bring your grin,
In this garden, fun shall begin!

Muse of the Meadow

In a field where daisies dance,
A snail learns to take a chance.
He slips and slides with quite the grace,
While munching leaves at a quick pace.

The butterflies throw a grand soiree,
With nectar flowing in wild display.
But frogs jump in, with all their might,
Creating quite the funny sight.

The bees are buzzing a jittery tune,
Chasing blossoms under the moon.
A squirrel giggles from high above,
Sprinkling laughter like seeds of love.

So join this merry, lively crew,
Where every bloom has something new.
In nature's circus, come take a seat,
Where joy and wits so often meet.

Enchanted Grove

In a grove where fruits hang low,
A monkey swings, putting on a show.
He takes a bite of a berry blue,
And ends up looking like a smurf too.

A parrot squawks, 'What a zest!'
While juggling lemons, he's quite the best.
A raccoon joins with a mask of fun,
Stealing snacks while he plays and runs.

The trees whisper secrets, oh so sly,
While squirrels debate who can reach the sky.
Each branch is an audience, taking bets,
On who can crack the funniest sets.

In laughter's realm, we find our place,
With goofy chants and wild embrace.
So revel here in silliness bright,
In this enchanted, whimsical night.

Dandelion Dreams

Dandelions dance in the breeze,
As a cat ponders on her knees.
She thinks of fish in the clouds above,
And how they'd taste—oh, the things she loves.

A bumblebee buzzes a clumsy tune,
Aiming for petals, but hits a raccoon.
With a startled jump and a playful roll,
They tumble together; that's how they stroll.

The petals puff out in winds that tease,
Each one a wish, carried with ease.
While grasshoppers hop in a mad charade,
Competing for laughs like it's a parade.

So blow on those seeds, let dreams take flight,
In the land where folly reigns day and night.
Join the fun, let your worries fade,
In a world of whimsy, let's play and invade.

Savoring Sun-kissed Memories

A peach falls down with a soft 'thud',
Causing ants to roll in a big, sweet flood.
They carry crumbs like they're gold,
Making each moment feel so bold.

Strawberries giggle as they squish,
While melons swing with a juicy swish.
Watermelon bursts with a splash of glee,
Creating a scene as messy as can be.

The grapes are gossiping, oh so grand,
They whisper tales of the berry band.
Each burst of laughter, a bubbling cheer,
As fruit-flavored fables fill the air.

So savor these memories, juicy and bright,
As nature's laughter ignites the night.
In the orchard's embrace, come join the cheer,
For a sun-kissed tale awaits you here.

Petals on the Path

A daisy tripped on its own head,
Laughing at how the tulips fled.
While roses dressed in silly hats,
Chasing bees and dodging cats.

A squirrel tried to take a swing,
But ended up in a flower ring.
Lilies giggled as they sway,
Singing songs in a breezy way.

Daffodils started a dance party,
Twirling around, oh so hearty.
They waved at passing butterflies,
Who winked back with bright surprise.

The sun chuckled at the scene,
With bees as dancers, swift and keen.
Nature's whimsy, a colorful path,
Where laughter blooms and teacups splash.

Unveiling Nature's Secrets

Behind the leaves, a secret plot,
Where mushrooms grow, and squirrels trot.
The grass whispers tales of the wise,
While daffodils share their secret fries.

At dawn, the sun peeks, what a show,
While bunnies bounce with a gleeful glow.
"Why is there dirt on your nose?" I tease,
"I was digging up dance moves from the breeze!"

Raccoons host late-night munching feats,
With pies made of acorns, oh such treats!
Every critter hums a different tune,
Under the magic of the silvery moon.

So take a stroll, lend an ear,
Listen close, there's charm to hear.
Nature giggles, blushing in humor,
As secrets unfold, it's quite the rumor!

Spirits of the Old Oak

The old oak tree knows all the tricks,
With branches that spin like circus flicks.
It tells tales of frogs with grand plans,
And squirrels that seek applause from fans.

"Hey! You there!" calls a cheeky crow,
"Your hair's as wild as the winds that blow!"
The oak sways, laughing deep inside,
Watching antics with giddy pride.

With every swing of its aged limbs,
It helps the earth celebrate whims.
"Let's host a party!" the mushrooms shout,
"Bring snacks and games, let's dance about!"

So under the leaves, a world of cheer,
Where antics and laughter fill the sphere.
The old oak chuckles, wise and spry,
As joy blooms like clouds in a bright sky.

Potpourri of Life's Lessons

Life's a salad, mix it well,
Throw in laughter, a touch of spell.
Add some quirks, a pinch of fun,
And don't forget your favorite pun.

Berries teach us not to fret,
While pickles say, "Don't you forget!"
Bananas slip, but rise with grace,
Smiling wide in this tasty race.

The carrots crunch with clumsy cheer,
Saying "Don't take life too near!"
While pumpkins boast of seeds they spread,
Whispering dreams yet to be fed.

So toss your worries with flair and zest,
In this potpourri, you'll find the best.
Nature's lessons, sweet and bright,
Blooming lessons, full of light!

Lush Landscapes of Care

In fields so green, a sight so grand,
A squirrel juggles nuts in hand.
The daisies dance, they spin and sway,
While bees in bowties buzz away.

A rabbit dons a tipsy hat,
Complaining 'bout a neighbor's cat.
The carrots gossip, roots entwined,
They plot escapes, they're quite refined.

The sun throws rays like silly darts,
While worms dig tunnels, acting arts.
A tomato dreams of being ripe,
But fears the salsa hype, oh gripe!

In this grand plot, what joy prevails,
Where laughter grows, and fun never fails.
With jests of nature, smiles abound,
In every quirk, pure joy is found.

Raindrops in Ripened Fields

Raindrops plop on a cabbage head,
A chorus sings of "let's be fed!"
Birds in hats, they serenade,
The sunflowers join the fun parade.

A puddle's splash, a muddy dance,
Potatoes plot their funky chance.
"Let's roll!" they cheer with muddy glee,
As worms do somersaults with spree.

Corn stalks whisper, 'Let's have a feast,'
But scarecrows look like they've been least.
A rain-soaked lettuce waves goodbye,
And dreams of dips that never lie.

With every drop, a giggle flows,
As nature's humor brightly glows.
In playful rains and happy squeals,
The joy of growth is all that heals.

Treasures of the Harvest

In baskets wide, where treasures dwell,
A pumpkin sings its squishy bell.
Zucchini struts in style so bold,
While eggplants wear their purple gold.

A melon tries to roll away,
But squash just laughs, "Come here and play!"
Tomatoes boast with red cheek pride,
While peppers dance, they're bonafide.

The harvest moon gives quite the show,
As veggies brace for chilly snow.
They tell tall tales of summer's sun,
Where carrots flexed and had their fun.

With every crop, a chuckle sprouts,
In garden jokes, there are no doubts.
Each quirky fruit, and veggie bright,
Makes every table a pure delight.

Emblems of Flora and Fauna

A dandelion dreams to be a star,
While ants march on, thinking they are.
The daisies gossip about the breeze,
Meanwhile the turtles take their ease.

A ladybug dons polka-dot flair,
While spiders throw their webs with care.
The butterflies in skirts of hue,
Flutter about, acting brand new.

Sunflowers wink at each passing bee,
In a field of giggles, wild and free.
While grasshoppers play their tiny tunes,
And ponder life beneath the moons.

In this patchwork of flora's charm,
Each cast of critters brings their balm.
With every laugh and twist of fate,
Nature's bounty is oh so great.

Boughs of Abundance

Apples giggle up in the tree,
Wobbling like a clown, so free.
A pear in shades of yellow blush,
Promising a lunch, oh what a rush!

Bananas practicing their dance moves,
Swinging wildly, oh how they groove.
Cherries in the mix, red as can be,
Whispering jokes, 'Come swing with me!'

Lemons zestfully squeeze out a laugh,
As orange slices share a witty gaff.
Kiwi jokes, a furry delight,
Have us rolling through the night!

Together they play, a fruity soirée,
Casting their silliness all through the day.
Nature's comedy, with giggles galore,
Living by laughter, who could want more?

Petals of Perseverance

In a bloom where daisies make a fuss,
A tulip trips, oh what a plus!
Roses chat about their finest scent,
While daffodils giggle, their petals bent.

Sunflowers stretch, reaching for the sky,
Swaying and laughing as bees buzz by.
A lily shoes a little less grace,
But the garden bursts with its fairness and pace.

When storms roll in, leaves flutter and flail,
Petals dance like they're telling a tale.
Through tangled weeds, the flowers press on,
Claiming their laughs since the dawn's first yawn.

Each flower a character in a play,
Dancing through troubles in their own way.
With perseverance wrapped in glee,
Blooming with humor, wild and free!

Tapestry of Tenderness

In a patch of blossoms, fuzzy bees land,
Playing tag with petals so grand.
A marigold winks, making a show,
While violets chuckle, 'We're in the know!'

Butterflies flutter, dressing just right,
Attending the party of color and light.
An ant tells a tale of its daily chore,
While roses blush deeper, craving folklore.

The sun gives a nod, a wink in return,
As blossoms giggle, together they learn.
Each petal a story, a giggle, a sigh,
Creating a quilt that could tickle the sky.

Tenderness wrapped with a side of fun,
In nature's embrace, on the run.
Together they thrive, together they cheer,
In this laughing garden, love is clear!

Orchard of Dreams

In a whimsical orchard where wishes take flight,
Trees sway with laughter, what a delight!
Fruit hangs like baubles, giggling away,
Mischief and dreams weave through the day.

Peaches whisper secrets, juicy and sweet,
While plums make puns about each passing beat.
Citrus fruit chuckles, its zest in the air,
Spreading the joy with an aromatic flair.

At dusk, when the fireflies start their dance,
Cherries dream up a fanciful chance.
Together they plot the next morning's glee,
In this orchard of dreams, come play with me!

With laughter in abundance, the fruits unite,
Creating a symphony, oh what a sight!
In a harvest of chuckles, wisdom is sown,
In this playful orchard, you're never alone!

Essence of Eden

In a paradise where bananas dance,
Apples giggle, taking a chance.
Pears wear hats, oh what a sight,
Grapes in pajamas, a jolly night.

Oranges play tag, rolling with glee,
Chasing the laughter, wild and free.
Berries sneak cookies, just for a taste,
In this garden, there's no time to waste.

Radishes prance in a petty ballet,
While carrots tell jokes in their funny way.
Beets in bowties, they twirl and spin,
Being root veggies, but all the same, win.

Here in this realm of mischief and cheer,
Every fruit and veggie, they hold dear.
So let's sow some laughter, let joy expand,
In this goofy Eden, oh so grand!

Blooms of Becoming

Petunias wearing shades, looking fly,
Sunflowers trying to reach the sky.
Daisies giggle at their own reflection,
While tulips boast of their fine complexion.

Zinnias juggling not just their bloom,
Violets getting lost, leaving more room.
Carnations whisper sweet, silly dreams,
In this garden of laughter, bursting at seams.

Chrysanthemums dance with a grace so odd,
Roses tell puns, they even applaud.
Lilies in tutus, they twirl with delight,
Each petal a joke that takes flight.

Blooming becomes a comedy show,
Where colors and scents steal the show.
So raise a glass to the blooms so bright,
In the garden of joy, everything feels right!

Elements of Nourishment

Carrots plotting a veggie parade,
While radishes bask in the sun's cascade.
Squash don their sunglasses, trying to chill,
As lettuce munches on dandelion's thrill.

Tomatoes are gossipers, juicy and bold,
Cucumbers twiddle, their stories unfold.
Beans in a race to the top of the vine,
While peas play hide and seek—what a design!

Zucchinis singing in their finest key,
Spinach in spandex, oh what a spree!
Sweet corn wearing jewels all aglow,
In this nourishing garden, banter does flow.

With every bite comes a laugh, you see,
In the harvest of humor, it's plain to agree.
So let's savor the blessings, one turnip at a time,
In this playful patch, life tastes like a rhyme!

Gardens of Reflection

Reflecting on life amid flowers and vines,
Cucumbers ponder, discussing designs.
Radishes think hard, they scratch their heads,
While daisies dream big in their cozy beds.

Butterflies chuckle at their own dreams,
Bees bragging 'bout honey and all that it seems.
Sunbeams tickle every petal around,
As nature indulges in laughter profound.

In this spot, squashes muse about fate,
While potatoes enjoy a leisurely state.
Even the weeds, with a grin, take a stand,
In this quirky garden, all go hand in hand.

So reflect on the joy, let silliness bloom,
As nature giggles, dispelling the gloom.
In this garden of laughter, all thrive afresh,
Every reflection, a giggle enmesh.

Whispers of the Weeping Willow

Beneath the branches, squirrels play,
Arguing over nuts all day.
A cat with dreams of becoming spry,
Chases shadows with a sigh.

The willow laughs, a gentle sound,
As leaves dance lightly on the ground.
With every gust, they take flight,
In the game of hide and seek, pure delight.

A frog hops in, bursting the fun,
Joined by a snail, they both try to run.
The grass ticks off the ants in line,
Counting them like stars that shine.

And as the sun dips low and bright,
Willow whispers secrets of the night.
A gathering of friends, oh what a sight,
In the garden, mischief feels so right.

Seasonal Harmony

Spring brings flowers, bright and gay,
Bees on a mission, buzzing away.
In summer's heat, the lemonade's sweet,
With watermelons, it's a fruity treat.

Autumn's leaves, all red and gold,
Pumpkin spice and tales retold.
Squirrels stash acorns for the cold,
As they discuss treasures worth their weight in bold.

Winter stirs a laugh or two,
As snowmen gather, wearing shoes.
A carrot nose, a scarf thrown wide,
With icicles dangling, full of pride.

Each season's jest, a playful dance,
Nature joins in, giving chance.
To revel in cycles, laughter loud,
In rhythms and antics, nature proud.

Hanging Gardens of Reflection

In a pot, a plant named Fred,
Once thought he could outgrow the bed.
He stretched and yawned, a leafy spree,
But only found he's stuck in me!

His neighbor, Sue, a jumpy fern,
Said, "Life's for fun; just take your turn!"
With roots that tangle, dance, and bend,
A friendship's formed, that won't quite end.

A bug named Larry, small but bright,
Flies in circles, oh what a sight!
He tells them tales of fields he flew,
While they both giggle, longing too.

So rooted deep in laughter's grace,
In pots of chaos, they find their place.
With every leaf, they tell a joke,
A verdant laugh from stem to yoke.

Roots of Connection

Down beneath the surface, they weave,
Roots entwined, no need to grieve.
"A little water, don't be shy!"
"Grow some more, let's reach for the sky!"

In the shade where gossip grows,
Underneath the soil's soft throws.
A budding flower spills the tea,
While worms just wiggle, oh so free.

A dandelion sneezes, "Bless you, friend!"
Spreading laughter that will never end.
"Let's make a wish and toss it high,
With petals dancing, oh me, oh my!"

And in the hush, they share and care,
Beneath the ground, a bond so rare.
In every twist, a joy displayed,
Roots of connection, happily laid.

Ephemeral Beauty

In the garden, things grow wild,
A pumpkin speaks with a giggling child.
Basil wears a tiny green hat,
While thyme just rolls over—how 'bout that?

Carrots dance beneath the moon,
Radishes hum a silly tune.
Peas in pods throw a funny fit,
While lettuce dreams of making a hit!

Threads of Green

Spinach spins around in glee,
Trying hard to escape the bee.
Zucchini races with a wink,
While tomato blinks and starts to think.

Cabbage laughs, then trips on thyme,
Squash tells jokes, but not in rhyme.
Everyone's part of the funny show,
In a patch where silly seeds do grow!

Splendor After Rain

Raindrops drip from leafy crowns,
As broccoli dons bright yellow gowns.
Carrots march with clever pride,
Twirling through the puddles, they glide.

Mushrooms giggle, doing a jig,
While peppers laugh, 'We're all so big!'
The sky clears up, they drink the sun,
In this post-rain dance, life is fun!

Abundance in Silence

In quiet spots, the herbs conspire,
Plotting mischief that does inspire.
Mint whispers secrets to the sky,
While sweet peas plot a seed-time lie.

Garlic grins, plotting a prank,
As onions laugh from the garden bank.
Each leaf has tales of antics grand,
In silence, they thrive, hand in hand!

Aroma of Forgotten Seasons

In the fridge, a pickle waits,
Hidden dreams and old debates.
The scent of cabbage fills the air,
Pasta whispers, 'Don't you dare!'

A jar of jelly, way past prime,
Claims it's just a taste of time.
Moldy bread, with crusty pride,
Says it's got nothing to hide.

Leftover pizza, a cheesy tale,
Three days old, but won't yet fail.
Dancing ants join round the plate,
This gourmet feast, our twist of fate.

So raise a glass of sour wine,
Laugh away, it's all divine.
Amidst the chaos, we shall thrive,
In this fridge, we're still alive!

Blossoms of Resilience

A cactus blooms with crooked flair,
In the bathroom, without a care.
Shower curtains swaying free,
Fashionable plants, oh can't you see?

A fern, it waves, quite full of sass,
Inviting dust, oh what a class.
That rubber tree, it claims it knows,
How to bloom in awkward rows.

With pots arranged in disarray,
The tulips giggle, come what may.
In their petals, bright and bold,
They share secrets, never told.

Through the chaos, they will dance,
Embracing nature's funny chance.
In this garden, wild and true,
Each blossom sings, "We thrive on you!"

Symphony of the Seasons

The autumn leaves perform a jig,
While winter wears a frosty wig.
Springtime blooms, all colors bright,
Summer's sun just can't be slighted.

The squirrels dance with acorn hats,
In rain boots, come the sloshy rats.
They sing a song of strange delight,
As seasons blur, with day and night.

A robin chirps, a comedic score,
While bunnies hop, and critics roar.
Cauliflower dreams of making stew,
But carrots laugh, "Not without me, too!"

And so it goes, the seasons play,
In this garden, they find their way.
A symphony of joy and cheer,
Each note reminds us, spring is near!

Echoing Dreams

In the garden, weeds take charge,
While dandelions sing at large.
The daisies chuckle, "We're still here!"
Invaders? Ha! We show no fear!

The gnomes gossip, tipsy from sun,
Debating which bug has more fun.
In this patch, they plot and scheme,
Weaving threads of silly dreams.

With worms wriggling, the soil's alive,
Each tumble brings a new high-five.
A scarecrow tells tales of delight,
Of fluffy clouds that zoom by night.

Beneath the stars, they sway and nod,
Finding magic in the odd.
In every corner, laughter beams,
As they chase down their echoing dreams!

Palette of Silent Growth

In the quiet plot, plants wear hats,
A carrot's grin, a squash that chats.
A tomato blushes, it's close to ripe,
While broccoli strikes a bongo-type!

Garden gnomes with their own DJ,
Spin celery records, dance all day.
With every sprout, some laughter flows,
Even weeds crack jokes, I suppose!

The tulips giggle in colorful rows,
Frisky as kittens, where sunlight glows.
Radishes wear shades like rock star spies,
While daisies gossip in flowery ties.

In this patch, the whispers are loud,
Mother Nature's quirks make her proud.
Take a stroll through this joyful scene,
Where veggies laugh, and no one's mean!

Growth's Gentle Melody

A lettuce croons in the morning light,
While peas hum tunes, oh, what delight!
Snapdragons chatter with bits of sass,
And daffodils giggle as squirrels pass.

The zucchini holds a secret feast,
With radishes, who laugh the most, at least.
Basil's serenade fills the air,
While chives whisper tales, in a delectably fair.

The beans sway to a lively beat,
Calling for carrots to tap their feet.
A compost pile, the best of jesters,
Turns old scraps into green ball-testers!

Even the sun joins in for fun,
Painting smiles on every one.
In this garden where giggles bloom,
Life's ripe with laughter, enough to consume!

Abundant Horizons

Behold the kale, in its curly stance,
Holding court like a veggie prince,
Onions chuckle, with eyes so round,
Telling stories of the wonders found.

Cucumbers stretch, trying to be cool,
Competing with radishes, who hide in the pool.
The cherries blush, as they sweetly tease,
Making pies giggle in summer's breeze.

A cornfield parade, on cob-like floats,
Jubilantly waving their golden coats.
Meanwhile, spinach offers a leafy cheer,
With beans skipping around, oh, so near!

From pumpkins who waddle to peppers that joke,
This garden's a circus, not just a poke.
Every harvest filled with playful glee,
Where nature's giggle is wild and free!

Dance of the Seasons

Spring twirls in, all dressed in green,
Flowers prance, a vibrant scene.
Bees do the hustle, nectar in hand,
While bunnies hop to the beat of the band.

Summer struts in, with swagger so bold,
Melons roll by, glistening gold.
Tomatoes boast with a sunlit grin,
While beetles breakdance on their shiny skin.

Autumn arrives with a rustling cheer,
Apples bobbing, those lucky dear.
Pumpkins strut with a glow so bright,
Holding lanterns to light up the night.

Winter sneaks in, with a snowflake swirl,
Carrots hide out as snowflakes whirl.
Even the frost finds joy to express,
In this garden, each season's a fest!

Roots Beneath the Surface

In the ground, they wiggle and squirm,
Potato jokes make the garden squirm.
Carrots whisper secrets in the dark,
While turnips giggle—oh, what a lark!

Worms hold debates on who's the best,
Potatoes claim they're above the rest.
But in this soil, they all have fun,
Dancing together, one by one.

The radishes blush, they keep it coy,
While onions bring sappy tales of joy.
In this patch, they banter and play,
Roots underfoot, having a grand ol' day!

So if you wander where the veggies thrive,
Remember their laughs, they feel so alive.
Don't take it too serious, just let it be,
In this garden, it's all about glee!

Petals of Passion

Blossoms flirt like they're on a date,
Bees buzzing close call it fate.
In the sun, they dance with delight,
Planting rumors all through the night.

Roses compete for the sweetest scent,
While daisies laugh at the time they spent.
Sunflowers strut with their heads held high,
Winking at clouds passing by in the sky.

Tulips tell tales of a bee mishap,
How it fell smack in a petals' lap!
Violets blush in the morning dew,
Sharing gossip, just a bloom or two.

In this floral rave, nothing is shy,
Petals whisper, "Oh my, oh my!"
Laughter erupts as they dance in a swirl,
Every flower's a unicorn in this floral world!

Sweetness in the Shadows

In the shade, fruits burst with cheer,
Bananas eavesdrop on gossip near.
Berries throw parties, oh what a scene,
Mangoes take selfies like queens and kings!

Grapes sit squished, sharing juicy lore,
Sour apples giggle and beg for more.
Citrus cracks jokes, they're a zestful bunch,
Lemons try puns over a chocolate crunch.

Peaches are smug, they roll their eyes,
While cherries form bands to reach the skies.
"Let's jam!" they shout, with a sugary tease,
Making paths sweeter than a summer breeze!

In this shadowy nook of delight,
Each piece of fruit shines so bright.
So if you wander into their spree,
Expect a tickle of fruit comedy!

Journey Through Orchard Paths

Strolling through rows of trees so grand,
Where apples hang by a ticklish hand.
Each leaf tells tales with a rustle and sway,
As critters pass by in a frolicsome way.

Orchards host fun, just watch your step,
Cider jokes led by branches adept.
Pears tease the wind while it tosses their hair,
Laughing as they sway with the fresh air.

Plums wear shades, trying to look cool,
Avoiding the bees like they're playing the fool.
A squirrel steals snacks, what a cheeky sight,
While acorns roll by in pure delight!

Each turn reveals fun, ripe for the find,
With stories that leave you tickled and blind.
So wander these paths, let laughter abound,
In each little corner, pure joy can be found!

Colorful Crescendos

In a patch of rhubarb, I met my fate,
A squirrel on a skateboard, oh what a trait!
He flipped over carrots, he soared through the beets,
While I laughed so hard, I tumbled from my seat.

Broccoli dancing, with a wig on its head,
Cauliflower giggles, while I chuckle instead.
Peas in their pods, throwing green confetti,
Life in this garden? Always loud and petty!

Pathways of Growth

Underneath cabbages, worms have a ball,
Throwing wild parties, they invite one and all!
Radishes are DJs, spinning tunes on the go,
While potatoes breakdance, putting on quite a show.

Tomatoes debating, who's redder, who's round,
Spinach joins in, making quite the sound.
Carrots in tutus, a ballet in bloom,
Shaking their roots, all the way to the moon!

Crescendo of Cultivation

In the plot of mischief, plots thicken 'round here,
Pumpkins play poker, whilst sipping on beer.
Zucchini in sunglasses, lounging with flair,
Waving at passersby, without a single care!

Garlic and onions, a smelly old fight,
Competing for space, well, that can't be right!
Onions are crying from laughter, it's true,
While garlic just smirks, knowing he'll outdo.

Fertile Imaginings

Lettuce with laughter, bubbling like soup,
Onions disguised as clowns, join in the loop.
Beets with bright smiles, red as can be,
Spreading good vibes, as sweet as can be.

Strawberries gossiping, on secrets they thrive,
'Berry' interesting tales! Oh, how they connive!
With fruits making puns, and herbs throwing fries,
In this wild wonder, even time complies!

Canvas of Continuity

In a field of laughter, seeds take flight,
Silly daisies twirl, oh what a sight!
Tomatoes wear shades, on a sunny day,
While carrots debate on which way to play.

Bees gossip sweetly, buzzing in tune,
Painting the air like a quirky cartoon.
Turnips in tuxedos, in a formal stance,
While pumpkins groove in a veggie dance.

Fragrant herbs chat, jiving with the breeze,
As rhubarb complains, 'I'm not here to freeze!'
Zucchini plays hide and seek, so sly,
'Where did it go?' Oh my, oh my!

On this canvas, laughter reaps its yield,
Life's merry circus sprawls across the field.
With every giggle, a new bud grows,
In this patch of joy where mischief flows.

Whispers of the Wind

The leafy trees chuckle, swaying along,
As dandelions dance to a breezy song.
Cherries provoke, 'Catch us if you can!',
While oranges giggle at their juicy plan.

The wind tells tales of veggies' delight,
As radishes wobble, preparing for flight.
Peas form a band, playing green tambourines,
While beets blush deeply, hiding behind greens.

Raspberry bushes throw a berry ball,
And strawberries say, 'We're having a ball!'
Sweet flourishes flutter, up in the sky,
Juggling the laughter as clouds drift by.

In the hush between whispers, joy starts to grow,
With giggles and twinkles, stealing the show.
Each breeze a promise, each laugh a send,
With a wink from nature, life's joys never end.

Cycle of Sunshine and Rain

The sun takes a bow, as the clouds roll in,
Raindrops giggle, ready to begin.
Splashing the soil, they throw a wild party,
While sunflowers crack jokes that are quite hearty.

'Here comes the drizzle!' the lettuce will shout,
And broccoli dances, shaking about.
Cucumbers slide in with a slick little grin,
While peppers pop jokes like they're wearing a fin.

Puddles become oceans for frogs leaping high,
And tomatoes burst forth with laughter in shy.
In this churn of weather, the fun never ends,
As veggies unite and the garden transcends.

A cycle of joy, of sass and of play,
With laughter as bright as the sun's best ray.
Through drizzle and sunshine, the humor remains,
In the garden of antics where happiness reigns.

Eden's Embrace

Here in the Eden where giggles collide,
Bananas wear hats as they pose with pride.
Apples drop puns from their leafy high ground,
While laughing in rhythm, the fruit dances round.

'Berry' excited, the strawberries cheer,
Pumpkins roll over, they're full of good cheer.
Cabbages gossip in leafy green chat,
While playful zinnias say, 'Check this out, Matt!'

The grapes hold a concert, so juicy and sweet,
Fruits sway to their rhythm, tapping their feet.
Every corner bursts with hilarious flair,
A garden where humor grows richly, we swear.

As blossoms bloom forth with smiles so wide,
In the embrace of the laughter, we all take pride.
Nature's a jester, with joy as her game,
A whimsical tapestry, all find their fame.

Echoes of a Growing Season

In springtime's grasp, we plant with glee,
Tomatoes dance, peas sing in spree.
Carrots wiggle, beans play peek-a-boo,
While cucumbers argue, 'Who's greener than you?'

Bumblebees buzz, the sun's a warm friend,
Radishes giggle, their roots they defend.
As squashes grow wide, they're feeling quite proud,
And radish tops whisper, 'We're part of the crowd!'

Oh, lettuce lays lazy in leafy delight,
While peppers turn red, it's quite the sight.
With each garden row, a chuckle will spread,
Silly seedlings turn rich soil to thread!

In harvest's embrace, we share in the fun,
With veggie-themed jokes, we've barely begun.
So gather 'round, friends, let laughter abound,
For in every sprout, a new giggle is found!

Blossoming Hope

In the garden of dreams where daisies arise,
A shy little worm wears a worm-sized disguise.
He wiggles and squiggles with terrible flair,
As butterflies giggle, saying, 'Who's that down there?'

The daisies, so cheerful, are dressed in their whites,
While sunflowers strut, having bold, lofty heights.
'We're reaching for the stars!' they all seem to shout,
But the carrots just chuckle, 'Let's not go out!'

A thrilling adventure, with each bud awake,
Tomatoes in sunglasses, 'Don't make us break!'
With humor and joy, they dance all around,
While beans throw confetti, laughing, 'We're crowned!'

As petals unfurl, and life's colors soar,
The garden, a stage, leaves us wanting more.
Where whimsy and giggles in bright blooms will cope,
We cultivate laughter and blossom with hope.

Cultivating Joy

In the potting soil, a party unfolds,
With herbs in the corner, acting so bold.
'Basil's the best!' claims the sweet little sprig,
While thyme rolls its eyes, saying, 'This is too big!'

Peppers are struttin', they're dressed to the nines,
While herbs share their secrets of cocktail designs.
Mint sips on water while fanning a leaf,
And rosemary's laughing, 'Isn't this brief?'

With a trowel in hand and mud on our face,
We plant silly seeds; this is our happy place.
Carrots play games, eager to hide,
Hiding away 'til their moment's applied.

To cultivate joy, all we need is a patch,
A sprinkle of laughter, it's quite the perfect match.
Beneath sunny skies, our garden will thrive,
With giggles and grins, we're truly alive!

Fruits of Reflection

In a mellow grove where the apples all joke,
A peach likes to prance, hoping no one will poke.
Hilarity blossoms, who's juiciest here?
Bananas all chuckle, hilariously near!

As shadows grow long, the berries give weigh,
"We're little yet mighty, find us in sweet play!"
Citrus claims sass with zest bursting bright,
While melons laugh loud and refuse to take flight.

Reflection time comes as raindrops gleam bright,
Nature's laughter here echoes through the night.
As fruits share their tales on a sweet summer's breeze,
We roll with the giggles like tall, swaying trees.

So let's toast with juices, each glass a delight,
To the fun-loving bounty, we'll savor tonight.
From kernels to pomes, we honor the cheer,
In reflections of fruit, let laughter be near!

www.ingramcontent.com/pod-product-compliance
Lightning Source LLC
Chambersburg PA
CBHW070005300426
43661CB00141B/241